A Carpenter

by Douglas Florian

Greenwillow Books New York

For my daughter Ariel

Black felt pen, crayon,
colored pencils, and
watercolor paints were
used for the full-color art.
The text type is
Bryn Mawr Book.

First Edition
10 9 8 7 6 5 4 3 2 1

Library of Congress
Cataloging-in-Publication Data
Florian, Douglas.
A carpenter / by Douglas Florian.
p.   cm.
Summary. A simple description
of what a carpenter does
in his daily work.
ISBN 0-688-09760-X.
ISBN 0-688-09761-8 (lib. bdg.)
1. Carpenters—Juvenile literature.
2. Carpentry—Juvenile literature.
[1. Carpenters.   2. Carpentry.
3. Occupations.]   I. Title.
TH5604.F58   1991
694'.092—dc20
90-30752   CIP   AC

A carpenter works with wood,

measuring it with his ruler,

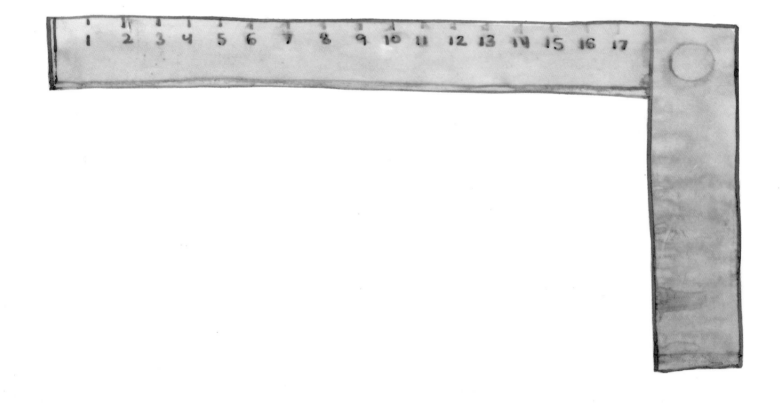

cutting it with his saw,

smoothing it with his plane,

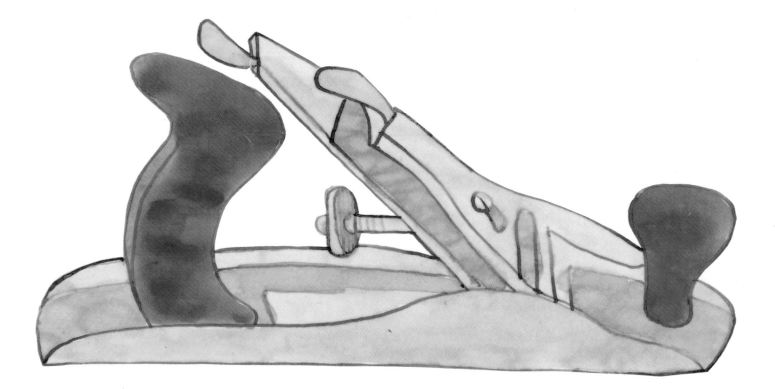

shaping it with
his mallet and chisel,

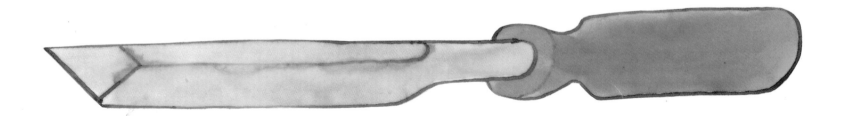

joining it with his hammer and nails,

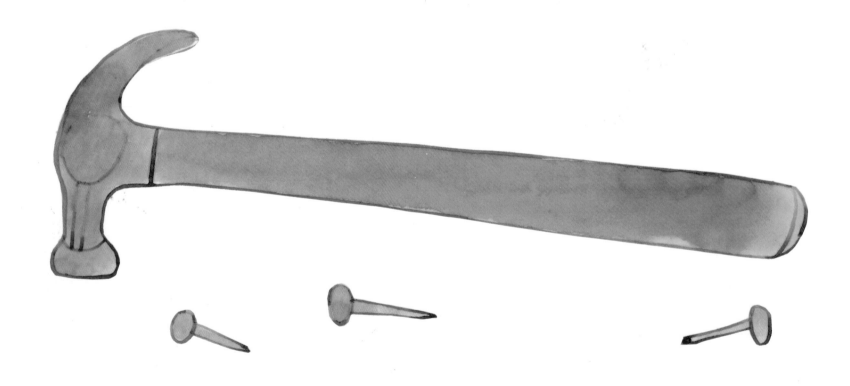

building things with his tools.

Walls and floors.

Windows and doors.

Shelves and stairs.

Tables and chairs.

Wooden sleds

and baby beds.

Day after day,

inside and out,

a carpenter works with wood.